ANIMAL MINDS

What Are They Thinking?

DANA L. CHURCH

ORCA BOOK PUBLISHERS

Text copyright © Dana L. Church 2024

Published in Canada and the United States
in 2024 by Orca Book Publishers.
orcabook.com

All rights reserved. No part of this publication may be reproduced or transmitted in any form or by any means, electronic or mechanical, including photocopying, recording or by any information storage and retrieval system now known or to be invented, without permission in writing from the publisher.

Library and Archives Canada Cataloguing in Publication
Title: Animal minds : what are they thinking? / Dana L. Church.
Names: Church, Dana L., author.
Series: Orca wild ; 12.
Description: Series statement: Orca wild ; 12 | Includes bibliographical references and index.
Identifiers: Canadiana (print) 20230198570 | Canadiana (ebook) 20230198589 | ISBN 9781459834156 (hardcover) | ISBN 9781459834163 (PDF) | ISBN 9781459834170 (EPUB)
Subjects: LCSH: Cognition in animals—Juvenile literature. | LCSH: Animal intelligence—Juvenile literature. | LCSH: Cognition in animals—Research—Juvenile literature. | LCSH: Animal intelligence—Research—Juvenile literature.
Classification: LCC QL785 .C58 2024 | DDC j591.5/13—dc23

Library of Congress Control Number: 2023934770

Summary: Part of the nonfiction Orca Wild series for middle-grade readers and illustrated with color photographs throughout, this book examines how animals think and the ways scientists study their cognition. Illustrated with photographs throughout.

Orca Book Publishers is committed to reducing the consumption of nonrenewable resources in the production of our books. We make every effort to use materials that support a sustainable future.

Orca Book Publishers gratefully acknowledges the support for its publishing programs provided by the following agencies: the Government of Canada, the Canada Council for the Arts and the Province of British Columbia through the BC Arts Council and the Book Publishing Tax Credit.

The author and publisher have made every effort to ensure that the information in this book was correct at the time of publication. The author and publisher do not assume any liability for any loss, damage, or disruption caused by errors or omissions. Every effort has been made to trace copyright holders and to obtain their permission for the use of copyrighted material. The publisher apologizes for any errors or omissions and would be grateful if notified of any corrections that should be incorporated in future reprints or editions of this book.

Front cover photo(s) by Anup Shah/Getty Images and Stuart Westmorland/Getty Images
Back cover photo by WhitcombeRD/Getty Images
Design by Jenn Playford and Dahlia Yuen
Edited by Kirstie Hudson

Printed and bound in South Korea.

27 26 25 24 • 1 2 3 4

How do sea turtles like this one know how to navigate in vast oceans to find food and nesting sites? Let's find out!
YFHISHINUMA/GETTY IMAGES

For Cia, with immense love and gratitude

Contents

Introduction 1

1
Same but Different:
Personality in Animals

Eight-Armed Individuals 5
What Is Personality? 6
Looking for Personality in Animals 7
Dolphins and the Big Five 11
From Tragedy to Opportunity 14
The Big Five and Other Animals 16
How Is Studying Personality Useful? 18

2
Where Did I Put My Banana?
Remembering Where Things Are

A Yummy Memory Test 26
What Is Spatial Memory? 29
A Face-Off for Hidden Food 31
How Do Animals Remember? 32
Putting It All Together 36
Shortcut Specialists 39

3
Easy as 1, 2, 3:
Counting in Animals

False Alarm! Just a Test	46
1, 2, 3 in Bees	48
Animals Using Numbers	50
What Does It Mean to Count?	54
"More" or "Less"	56
What's the Verdict? Can Animals Count?	60

4
Figure It Out!
Animals Solving Puzzles

Innovative Vultures	66
Puzzle Boxes	68
The Floating Object Task	70
The Aesop's Fable Task	72
Windows into Other Minds	75
The Future of Animal Cognition	79

Glossary	82
Resources	84
Acknowledgments	86
Index	88

Bumble bees like to keep to themselves. This one is too busy drinking nectar and gathering pollen from flowers to bother with people.
GARY MAYES/GETTY IMAGES

Introduction

One summer I got a job working with bumble bees. I had to catch wild bumble bees and watch their behavior as they flew in an indoor screened cage. I was terrified. I thought, What am I doing? I'll be stung every day! But as a university student, I was desperate for summer employment.

I soon realized that bumble bees are not stinging machines ready to pounce on human flesh. They are too busy gathering food (nectar and pollen) from flowers to feed the hundreds of bees in their family, looking after all the eggs that will hatch into new bees and keeping their nest tidy. They keep to themselves. I started to relax.

Part of my job was to run experiments that involved fake flowers. All the flowers looked the same. However, in some of the flowers there was nectar, which was water mixed with table sugar. This nectar had no scent, so the only way the bees could find the nectar-filled flowers was by memorizing their locations. Well, the bumble bees figured this out fast. Their memories were impressive. For the rest of the summer, every time I gave the bees new tests with the fake flowers, they passed with flying colors. I had no idea they are little problem-solvers.

As we will see, a lot goes on in the mind of this bumble bee and in the minds of other animals.
RUTH HIGGINSON

Cognition comes from a Latin word meaning "to know."

I also learned that no two bees are alike. There were big differences between *foragers*—bees that collect food. Some were superstars, foraging nonstop every day, flying lightning fast in a straight line back and forth between the flowers and the nest. Others were slower and didn't forage as often. Then there were those who left the nest and couldn't find their way back. I had to pick them up gently with a long pair of tweezers and place them back in the nest. I realized I had assumed all bees were copies of one another and behaved the same way. Instead, there are individual differences among bees.

The professor I worked for that summer studied *animal cognition*—how animals learn, remember, make decisions and solve problems. She studied how animals think. I had no idea scientists could spend their careers studying that. I was hooked! I decided to study animal cognition too. It opened up a whole new world for me that I want to share with you. Although I can't fit the entire world of animal cognition into this book, I thought we could explore how scientists tackle questions like, Do dolphins have personalities? Can lions count? So settle in, get comfy, and let's explore the minds of other animals.

> Humans are animals too! In this book, humans and animals are referred to separately to keep things clear and simple.

Have you ever visited an animal in a petting zoo? Have you wondered what they could be thinking about as you held them?
SOLSTOCK/GETTY IMAGES

Not all octopuses react the same way. This octopus appears quite bold, whereas others might be timid and swim away.
STUART WESTMORLAND/GETTY IMAGES

1

Same but Different
Personality in Animals

Scientist Jennifer Mather opened the lid of the aquarium. She leaned over, the tip of her nose almost touching the surface of the water. She peered down and looked straight into the eye of…an octopus. The octopus's black slit of a pupil grew large. The octopus crawled along the bottom of the tank, its eight suckered arms stretching, curling and uncurling. Mather watched until it came to rest in a far corner. She lowered a prickly test-tube brush into the water and gently touched one of the octopus's arms. *POOF!* An explosion of black ink. The dark cloud dissolved, and the octopus was nowhere to be seen. Mather knew it was hiding in a black plexiglass box on the bottom of the aquarium. She set the test-tube brush on the table beside her and wrote some notes.

EIGHT-ARMED INDIVIDUALS

What was Mather doing, besides annoying an octopus? She was giving it a **personality** test. The first part is the alert test. As we just saw, you open the lid of the aquarium and lean over so the octopus can see you.

How does the octopus react? Does it crawl away? Change color? Dip its head down? Or something else? Next is the threat test, where you gently tap one of the octopus's legs with a brush. Again, what does the octopus do? Does it squirt a cloud of ink? Does it zip away by jet propulsion? Some octopuses grab the brush with their arms! Finally there is the feeding test, where you drop a crab into a corner of the tank. Does the octopus eat the crab right away? How does the octopus approach and attack it?

In the early 1990s, Mather gave this personality test to many octopuses. She found that some octopuses are more active than others, some act more anxiously and others are calmer. Some are bold and approach new things, whereas others avoid them. With her colleague Roland Anderson, Mather organized these personalities into three components: activity, reactivity and avoidance. At the time, these components were not much different from the ones that were used to describe the differences between human babies!

If octopuses have individual personalities, what about other animals? If you have a pet, like a cat, dog or bird, I'm sure you can easily describe what they're like. But can we call our descriptions *personalities*?

Octopuses, such as this one, have shown evidence that they have their own personality.
JACKIE HILDERING, THEMARINEDETECTIVE.COM

WHAT IS PERSONALITY?

Personality refers to how each human tends to behave over time and in different situations. Each person is different, but we can see similarities in people's behavior too. For decades psychologists puzzled over the question, What is the best way to describe all the individual differences people show? In the 1930s psychologists gave people long lists of adjectives that describe **traits**, such as *talkative*, *brave*, *patient* and *messy*. Then they asked them to rate to what degree each adjective described themselves, on a scale from *extremely inaccurate* to *extremely accurate*. Later, in the 1980s, psychologists determined that these traits could be best organized into five groups, or factors. The names they gave to these five factors are *extroversion*, *agreeableness*, *conscientiousness*, *openness* and *neuroticism*.

This theory of personality has stood the test of time, and the questionnaire based on it is famously known as the Big Five. The main idea is that every person's unique personality can be described using these five factors. Each factor is on a spectrum—you can be high, you can be low, or you can be somewhere in between. The combination of where you are in each of the five factors describes who you are.

To help remember the names of the Big Five, the first letters can be arranged to spell *ocean* or *canoe*.

LOOKING FOR PERSONALITY IN ANIMALS

Unfortunately, we can't ask animals to answer a series of questions about themselves or rate adjectives. (I wish I could ask my dog or bumble bees questions from the Big Five, like, Do you make friends easily? Do you like to tidy up? Do you dislike change?) However, we can give animals a series of tests and see how they react. This lets us see individual differences in behavior. We saw this earlier with the octopuses. We can also watch animals over time in their natural environment and see if there are patterns in how each individual behaves in different situations. Another strategy is to ask people who are familiar with the animals, like zookeepers and pet owners, to fill out a questionnaire like the Big Five for each animal they know.

My friend Leann has a beautiful, fluffy cat named MacGyver. MacGyver is cautious when meeting new people, but then he can be quite affectionate. MacGyver certainly seems to have his own personality.
LEANN HARVEY

Where Do You Fit in the Big Five?
The Factors and What They Mean

FACTOR NAME	WHAT DOES IT MEAN?
EXTROVERSION: What energizes you? How do you interact with others?	If you are high in extroversion, you feel recharged after being with people, and you often seek out the company of others. People high in extroversion (called **extroverts**) are often referred to as the "life of the party." On the other end of the spectrum is introversion. People who are *introverts* feel tired after interacting with others and recharged after being alone. Introverts are often described as quiet and thoughtful.
AGREEABLENESS: How do you get along with others?	If you tend to be polite, kind, affectionate and sensitive to other people's needs, you are high in agreeableness. People low in agreeableness tend to be blunt, ill-tempered and sarcastic, and do not leave people with a warm, fuzzy feeling.
CONSCIENTIOUSNESS: Can you control yourself and behave in ways that are socially acceptable?	People who are high in conscientiousness show strong self-discipline, follow the rules and plan and organize. If you tend to procrastinate (put things off until later) and be impulsive, you would score lower on this spectrum.
OPENNESS: Do you like to learn and try new things? Do you have a vivid imagination?	If you do, you are probably high in openness. People who are lower in openness tend to prefer routine over variety, stick to what they know and avoid abstract ideas.
NEUROTICISM: How confident are you? Do you often feel anxious or worry a lot?	People high in neuroticism tend to be anxious, sad, self-conscious—they worry a lot and doubt their abilities. Those who score low in neuroticism tend to be confident and brave and don't worry very much.

Personality is still a huge and important topic in psychology. There are still a lot of unanswered questions about what makes each of us who we are.

An advantage of using a personality questionnaire that was designed for humans, like the Big Five, is that it allows us to compare people with other animals. It also lets us make comparisons between other species. However, some of the questions need to be changed so that they are appropriate for the animal in question. For example, it would be hard for a zookeeper to answer some of the questions from the Big Five, such as, Does Charles the gorilla like big parties? Does Charles have a vivid imagination?

Charles is a male silverback gorilla who lives at the Toronto Zoo. He is the star of a research study we'll see later in this book.

Based on how excited this dog looks, you might say it is high in extroversion and agreeableness.
CATHERINE FALLS COMMERCIAL/GETTY IMAGES

Do dolphins have their own personalities?
IRINA NO/SHUTTERSTOCK.COM

People and trainers who work closely with dolphins often notice individual differences in their behavior.
KALI9/GETTY IMAGES

DOLPHINS AND THE BIG FIVE

In the early 2000s, Lauren Highfill was a student studying dolphins at the Marine Life Oceanarium in Gulfport, Mississippi. As she watched and made notes on the dolphins' behaviors, she noticed that the dolphins were not all the same. Some dolphins seemed a bit more playful, for example, while others seemed a bit pushier and more dominant. Highfill and her supervisor, scientist Stan Kuczaj, suspected that these differences might be signs that each dolphin has its own personality. They decided to do an experiment to find out. They revised the wording of the Big Five test so that it reflected dolphin behavior. Highfill and Kuczaj then asked students and trainers to use this revised test to judge each of the 16 dolphins at the Marine Life Oceanarium. Each of these judges had known the dolphins for at least one year. They completed the test for each dolphin on their own and did not discuss the test with one another. For every adjective in the test, the judges had to rate each dolphin on a scale of 1 to 7, where 1 was "very accurate description" and 7 was "very inaccurate description."

A Personality Test for Dolphins
Developed by Lauren Highfill and Stan Kuczaj

EXTROVERSION

Assertive: is not easily intimidated

Playful: shows play behavior

Active, energetic: moves around a lot (swimming, leaping, breaching)

Timid: is hesitant, shy

Quiet: does not vocalize often

Unexcitable: is not easily roused to action; relatively unresponsive

AGREEABLENESS

Friendly, gentle: responds to others in an easy, kind manner; not hostile

Obedient: obeys and cooperates with trainers' instructions

Affiliative, companionable: appears to like the company of others; seeks out social contact with another animal or person

Inflexible: is stubborn, not willing to adapt or change

Demanding: requires much effort or attention from other dolphins and/or humans

Selfish: is self-centered or concerned mostly with itself and its needs

CONSCIENTIOUSNESS

Careful, cautious: shows care in its actions

Alert, attentive: appears to pay attention to its surroundings

Diligent: monitors its actions and shows a willingness to please

Lazy: resists work or exertion

Unreliable: cannot be depended on to do things

Inconsistent: is not predictable

OPENNESS

Creative, imaginative: uses new ways to approach situations and problems (for example, finds different ways to play with a toy)

Intelligent: learns easily and is quick to understand

Curious: is interested in new situations or objects

Not exploratory or inquisitive: doesn't seek out or investigate new situations or objects

Unoriginal, conforming: does not behave in new or unusual ways

Simple: displays behaviors that are routine and do not show much complexity

NEUROTICISM

Jealous: is resentful or envious of another dolphin

Aggressive: threatens or causes harm; rakes, bites or hits other animals and/or humans often

Temperamental: shows frequent mood swings

Relaxed, calm: is at ease; not tense or highly sensitive

Comfortable: is content; appears free from anxiety

Tolerant and easygoing: is often relaxed

Each dolphin was rated by three or more judges. When Highfill and Kuczaj looked at all the ratings, they found that the judges had rated each dolphin similarly, and each dolphin had its own unique score. This suggests that the 16 dolphins each had their own personality. For example, Sandy was the most open and conscientious of the dolphins, and Terri was the most agreeable. Naia was the most extroverted, and Jonah was the most neurotic.

Dolphin personalities were stable even after the stressful event of Hurricane Katrina. These dolphins were kept safe and happy after being rescued by the United States Navy.
CHRIS GETHINGS/WIKIMEDIA COMMONS/ PUBLIC DOMAIN

FROM TRAGEDY TO OPPORTUNITY

Remember that to show personality, an individual needs to behave in a consistent way over time and in different situations. For example, ever since I was a kid, I've been a cautious person (an element of the conscientiousness factor), regardless of where I am. To see whether the dolphins still had their unique differences over time, Highfill and Kuczaj planned to ask the judges to rate the dolphins again one year later. However, nature had other plans.

In August 2005 Hurricane Katrina slammed into Gulfport, Mississippi. It destroyed Marine Life Oceanarium. Eight of the dolphins were relocated to a safe place before the hurricane hit, but eight were still in one of the pools. Thankfully, these dolphins escaped into the Mississippi Sound and were later rescued. For a while they were kept in hotel swimming pools and pools provided by the United States Navy. Eventually all the dolphins were relocated to a large, open ocean pool at Atlantis Resort, Bahamas. Sadly, one dolphin did not survive. The rest did, however, which is nothing short of incredible.

Nine months after the dolphins were brought to Atlantis, they seemed to have settled into their new home. Highfill and Kuczaj started thinking again about their experiment. What if they asked the dolphins' new trainers at Atlantis to rate each dolphin using their Big Five personality test? If these new trainers rated the dolphins similarly to how the original judges had rated them, this would show that dolphins have stable personalities over time and across situations—even after traumatic, stressful events.

Three judges rated each dolphin using the Big Five test. Once again the judges' ratings were similar for each dolphin, showing that each dolphin had its own unique personality. Moreover, these new ratings matched the ratings given by the original judges. This means that each dolphin's uniqueness remained over time and under vastly different circumstances—the true test of personality.

Smart Thinking!

How We Think about Animals

How scientists view animals has changed over time. For example, in the 1800s, Charles Darwin presented his **theory of evolution** by **natural selection**. Darwin blew the top off scientific thinking at the time by arguing that humans are *not* fundamentally different from other animals—all living creatures are the product of evolution, and as a result, communication, intelligence and thought can be found throughout the animal kingdom. To fully understand the human mind and where it came from, we need to study the cognition of other animals. Darwin might be considered the first animal-cognition scientist. Today people are more accepting of the idea that animals have thoughts and minds of their own. As scientists discover more, will the way we think about animals change? If so, how?

THE BIG FIVE AND OTHER ANIMALS

Research in animal personality exploded in the 1990s and early 2000s. Scientists found that the Big Five personality factors could be used to describe the personalities of animals as diverse as chimpanzees, gorillas, rhesus monkeys, vervet monkeys, hyenas, dogs, cats, donkeys, pigs, rats, guppies and octopuses. Scientists continue to study animal personality today. Depending on the species of animal, there now are models besides the Big Five and a variety of different personality tests. The range of animals that show evidence of personality continues to grow, with recent additions being elephants, cats, sea lions, killer whales and amphibians such as frogs, toads, salamanders and newts.

Scientists in Australia found that the personality of pet ferrets can be structured using four dimensions they call *extroversion*, *sociability*, *attentiveness* and *neuroticism*. Sounds similar to the Big Five model originally designed for humans, doesn't it?
ERMOLAEVA OLGA 84/SHUTTERSTOCK.COM

Smart Thinking!

Different Ways of "Bee-ing"

There are individual differences between bumble bees. For instance, when the bees in our lab were ready to leave their nest box to find food, and I didn't lift up the gate right away, some bees would literally jump up and down. Some bees tried to crawl under the gate, whereas others turned around, went back into the nest and tried again later. Were the bees who jumped up and down more anxious or impatient? Were the bees who went back into the nest more "chill"?

In 2008 a team of scientists from Queen Mary University of London, England, presented bumble bees with flowers the bees had never seen before. This was meant to test the bees' reactions to new things, since behavior toward new things is one aspect of personality. Some bees approached the new flowers relatively quickly, whereas others were more hesitant. After a few days these individual differences disappeared. The scientists are not sure why. Remember that behavior patterns must be consistent over time in order to be evidence of personality. Do bumble bees not have personality? Maybe reaction to new things is not the best way to investigate bumble bee personality. Or maybe bumble bee personality is more short-term. This last idea is interesting considering that bumble bees have a pretty short life span compared with humans and other animals. (Worker bumble bees generally live for one to four weeks.)

Experiments like these show that it's possible to study personality in an animal like a bee, and they also help us understand bees at a deeper level. We can learn how to better help bees survive as well as understand more deeply what personality is in the first place.

HOW IS STUDYING PERSONALITY USEFUL?

The study of animal personality has improved animal welfare. Zoos now adjust enclosures to best suit the personalities of the animals living there. For example, if some individuals are shy, zoos provide them with more hiding places. If other individuals are more social, zoos give them space to hang out together. Sometimes new animals are added to zoos or transferred from one zoo to another. Zookeepers take the individual personalities of the animals into account so that there is a smooth introduction and the newcomer will fit in.

There is still much to discover and learn about animal personality. For instance, scientists don't know whether animals are born with a specific personality or whether it develops over time. Maybe it depends on the species. If you can think of questions about animal personality and how to find the answers, then you are on your way to becoming an animal-cognition scientist!

Just as some people are not suited for certain jobs, some dogs are not suited for certain jobs. This includes being a family pet. Sometimes people surrender dogs to shelters because its personality is too extroverted or "high energy." These dogs often make great working dogs. For example, their extroversion and energy can be put to good use tracking endangered species.

Dio was surrendered to an animal shelter for being too "high energy." Now he is a working conservation dog, helping scientists track orca pods in the Salish Sea by using his sharp nose to scent their poop on the water.
ISABELLE GROC

Providing zoo animals with enrichment, like this ball roped to a tree, can benefit their health and stimulate their natural behaviors. Animal personality research can help zookeepers decide what kind of enrichment is best and how to introduce it.
LINGUNGUN/SHUTTERSTOCK.COM

Anthropomorphism

Smart Thinking!

The word *anthropomorphism* comes from the Greek *anthropos*, meaning "human," and *morph*, meaning "form."

Anthropomorphism is the tendency to see other animals as humans or describe animals using human characteristics. Mickey Mouse and SpongeBob SquarePants are examples of animals who are anthropomorphized. Last time I checked, mice and sea sponges do not wear pants, walk on two legs and talk! That's what humans do. You can probably think of many other examples where the animals in books and cartoons act like people.

Anthropomorphism makes for good stories and entertainment. It is also easy to anthropomorphize our pets. When my kids leave for school, for example, our dog, Spirit, lies on her bed, looking out the window. I think, Aw, Spirit looks so sad! She must miss Lelynd and Lexi. But that is how *I* would feel in that situation. Maybe Spirit does miss my kids, or maybe she is experiencing nothing like "missing" at all. Maybe she is simply looking out the window.

Anthropomorphism can be a problem because it explains animal behavior using only a human perspective. It ignores the possibility that the animal experiences the world differently than we do. Animal-cognition scientists try very hard to recognize the role that anthropomorphism may play in their work. However, anthropomorphism can also be an important part of science. It can lead to questions and hypotheses that can be tested, like the personality tests we saw earlier. If you notice anthropomorphism, can you think of how it could be framed as a question that scientists could pursue?

Tigers, leopards and other big cats lead solitary lives. Lions live in groups called *prides*. If lions are more social, do they have a different personality structure compared with other species of cats?
PAUL SOUDERS/GETTY IMAGES

Scientist Spotlight

Lauren Highfill

Professor of Psychology and Animal Studies
Eckerd College, Florida

Lauren Highfill studies the cognition of a variety of species including dolphins, elephants, lemurs and dogs.

When did you first become interested in studying dolphin cognition?

It wasn't really until college, when I took an animal-behavior class, and it really just opened my eyes to the world of psychology through the lens of animals. I didn't know that you could study that. So that kind of turned things around for me.

Did the dolphins ever do anything funny?

The dolphins at Marine Life Oceanarium loved playing ball. We'd often throw the ball with them, but we were supposed to be there to do research, and so we'd be serious with our clipboard. The dolphins would try to get our attention. We would often get nailed in the head with a ball. They were like, "I'm here! I want to play with you!" We actually turned that into a ball-tossing experiment. We tested the dolphins where we faced them or faced away, to see if they would only throw it if we were looking at them. We found that if we were looking away, some of the dolphins would throw the ball harder.

What advice do you have for kids who are interested in studying dolphins?

The biggest thing is to try to get experience. You can volunteer at rescue-rehab types of facilities, or on some of those boat-based surveys that study wild dolphins. Or you can volunteer at an aquarium that houses dolphins. But getting any kind of animal experience is helpful. A lot of the skills that you use for studying horses, dogs or zoo animals can transfer over to work with marine mammals.

What does this lemur know and think about? What about dolphins, elephants or dogs? Scientists like Lauren Highfill are trying to find out.

SMITHLANDIA MEDIA/GETTY IMAGES

Do these gorillas remember where to find good food in their environment?
ERNI/SHUTTERSTOCK.COM

2

Where Did I Put My Banana?

Remembering Where Things Are

Suzanne MacDonald hid behind some dense shrubs. She heard a clang and a humming sound as a set of sliding steel doors opened nearby. Her heart quickened. She stared through the fence into the outdoor enclosure, waiting. A hulking dark figure slowly came into view. MacDonald held her breath. It was Charles, the Toronto Zoo's silverback western lowland gorilla.

Charles stood near the doors, his arms down, leaning on his knuckles. MacDonald could smell his musky wildness. He was staring ahead as if surveying his surroundings. He gave a quick snort, then galloped to the center of the enclosure. He picked up a blue plastic container. He took off the lid just as MacDonald had shown him how to do a couple of days earlier as he'd watched her through the fence. Charles reached inside, grabbed a handful of raisins and shoved them into his mouth. Charles loved raisins.

Tossing the empty container aside, Charles moved on. He soon found another blue container just like the first one. He opened it, ate the raisins inside and tossed that container too. Charles had soon found all eight containers that MacDonald had hidden. The sliding steel doors opened, and the rest of the gorilla troop bounded into the outdoor enclosure. For the rest of the day, they all used the plastic containers as toys.

A YUMMY MEMORY TEST

MacDonald played this game with Charles once a day for four more days. Each day the eight raisin-filled containers were in the same spots. Charles quickly learned where the containers were. She noticed that Charles followed a pattern. He always galloped to the center of the enclosure, found the container closest to him and then moved in a clockwise direction to find the others. He never went back to a previous spot. MacDonald wondered if the empty containers Charles flung to the ground reminded him where he had already been.

Then she gave Charles a harder task. Four of the eight containers had raisins, and the other four were empty. The containers with raisins were always in the same places. Charles had to find the four raisin-filled containers and remember where they were.

It didn't take long for Charles to learn where the raisin-filled containers were and avoid the empty containers. Charles also did something amazing. When he was learning where the four raisin-filled containers were, he picked up the containers and shook them. That way he didn't have to open the containers to see if they had raisins. No one had shown Charles how to do that. Go, Charles!

When wild animals like gorillas find fruit or plants that are not yet ready to be eaten, they can use their spatial memory to return to them later, when the fruit or plants are ripe and juicy.

Sometimes MacDonald would wait one or two weeks before giving Charles the game again. Even after such a long delay, his memory for the four locations was excellent. Another thing MacDonald noticed was that Charles always stopped searching after finding the fourth raisin-filled container. Was he counting?

Charles, a gorilla at the Toronto Zoo, aced Suzanne MacDonald's spatial memory experiment.
THE TORONTO ZOO

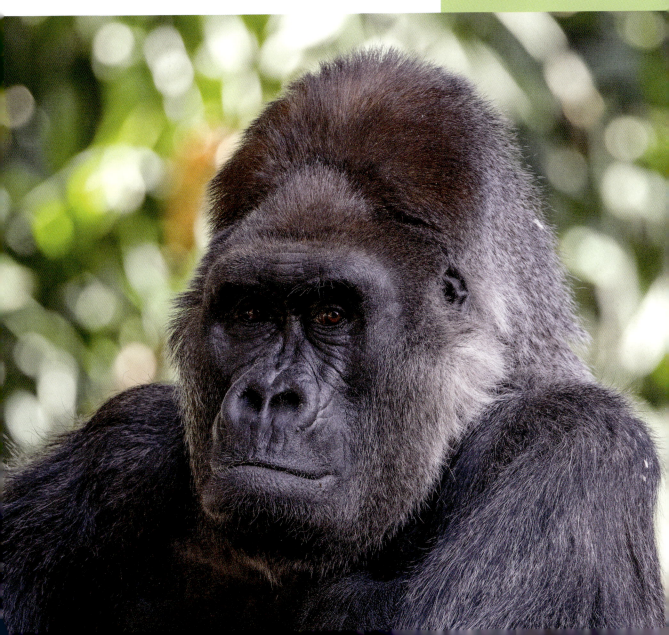

Sea Turtle Memory

These turtles are wearing removable tracking devices so scientists can learn how they navigate in the water. KENNETH LOHMANN

Sea turtles travel thousands of miles across the sea and then choose specific locations to feed and make their nests. Scientists think sea turtles might use one group of strategies to travel across the sea, such as detecting the magnetic fields of the earth and/or using the angles of sunlight through the water. Then, to locate a specific island or spot on a beach, the turtles might use the sound of waves crashing against land, beach smells, wave patterns in the ocean as the water moves around a land mass, or something else. They might also see some specific feature about the island that attracts them. Coastlines seem to be important to sea turtles. After scientists moved them off their path, the turtles often reoriented by swimming to a nearby coastline and following it until they arrived at the nesting site they were originally going to.

WHAT IS SPATIAL MEMORY?

MacDonald was studying Charles's *spatial memory*. Spatial memory is remembering where things are in the physical environment. This type of memory is very important for animals, because it lets them remember where their homes are and where food is. MacDonald suspected that western lowland gorillas have excellent spatial memory because in the wild they travel long distances to find food. Charles certainly seemed to have good spatial memory. But what if he was a gorilla genius? MacDonald needed to test other gorillas too. She also wondered if gorillas keep track of where others have eaten, because gorillas live in groups. Like any good scientist, MacDonald designed another experiment.

Puppe, an orangutan at the Toronto Zoo, also took part in a spatial memory task. Puppe and other orangutans were very good at remembering where banana-filled containers were placed. Like Charles, they searched using a pattern.
THE TORONTO ZOO

This time she placed food at 16 different spots in the Toronto Zoo's indoor and outdoor gorilla enclosures. Each spot, or "food site," had a green metal tube with a treat inside—one Kellogg's Frosted Mini-Wheat. Each morning before the zoo opened to the public, all the gorillas waited in their usual holding area, eating their breakfast of fruits and vegetables. While they were munching, MacDonald let two gorillas into the indoor and outdoor enclosures at the same time. As in the experiments with Charles, at first all 16 food sites had a Mini-Wheat. Later only half of the sites had one, and the gorillas had to remember where they were. There were two gorillas looking for the Mini-Wheats at once. What happened?

Wild gorillas appear to have good knowledge of their environment so they don't have to search randomly for food.
ANUP SHAH/GETTY IMAGES

A FACE-OFF FOR HIDDEN FOOD

It was always a full-on competition. The gorillas always split up and tried to find as many Mini-Wheats as possible. If they arrived at a site at the same time, they often slapped or pushed each other away. One gorilla named Josephine often sat on the food sites so the other gorilla couldn't get at them!

Overall, the gorillas remembered where the Mini-Wheats were, and they avoided visiting sites where they had already been. Each also avoided sites where the *other* gorilla had been. MacDonald noticed that while they were searching, the gorillas tended to watch each other. Like Charles, the gorillas often moved to the food site nearest to the one they were just at. However, they adjusted their pattern if the next site had already been visited by the other gorilla. Interestingly, when all the Mini-Wheats had been found, the pair of gorillas would line up by the door to be let back into the holding area. It was as if they were saying, "Hey, guys! We're done!" Were they counting the Mini-Wheats?

Later a team of scientists based in the United States followed a troop of wild gorillas for 10 months in their natural environment at the Mondika Research Center, located on the border between the Central African Republic and the Republic of the Congo. The scientists analyzed the gorillas' travel patterns and discovered that the gorillas moved very efficiently between their main area, food sites and even throughout less familiar areas. They did not travel in random directions but rather seemed to remember where something was and were able to calculate the best route to get there. As MacDonald suspected, gorillas seem to have a very detailed spatial memory.

Western lowland gorillas, like this juvenile male, live in some of Africa's most dense and remote rainforests.
ANUP SHAH/GETTY IMAGES

HOW DO ANIMALS REMEMBER?

How do animals remember where things are? Scientists discovered that animals use a number of strategies:

Search Patterns

Sometimes animals look for things by moving continuously in a particular way. We saw such *search patterns* with Charles and the other gorillas. They moved to the site closest to the one they were at, sometimes in a clockwise direction.

Beacons

These are sights, smells, sounds or other signals close to where the animal wants to go. Beacons are like someone waving and calling, "Hey, over here!" For example, the smell of a mother hamster's nest and the sounds of her babies can act as beacons for her to find her way back home. Flowers can act as beacons for bees, butterflies, hummingbirds and other animals who drink nectar. However, the animal has to be within range of the beacon to perceive it.

When some species of dung beetle find a fresh pile of dung (poop), they dig a burrow nearby and then roll balls of the dung back to this new home to eat later (yuck!). Scientists discovered that these dung beetles use *dead reckoning* to find their way from the dung pile to their burrow. Not only that, the beetles lean their heads down, stick their butts in the air and roll the balls of dung with their hind legs. In other words, they travel backward. Imagine doing a handstand, rolling a big ball with your legs and finding your way home!

EMILY BAIRD

Dead Reckoning

Some animals, after wandering around in many directions, travel back home in a straight line. I've seen bumble bees do this, and it's quite amazing. They calculate the distance and direction of all the little paths they took to create a route that leads them straight home—a process called *path integration*. Scientists discovered that desert ants use dead reckoning too. When ants were about to head back to their nest, the scientists moved them to a different spot. The ants traveled the same distance and direction that would have led them home. But the nest wasn't there.

The ants began searching around and around in an ever-expanding spiral. They never gave up! Eventually the scientists put the ants out of their misery by picking them up and placing them at the hole to their nest.

The Sun, Moon and Stars

Many animals use the sun to figure out which direction to go. **Nocturnal animals** (animals that are active at night) can use the moon and stars. Many species of small songbirds use the stars to navigate when migrating at night. Scientists tested this by placing the birds in a planetarium where they could adjust the movement of the stars and see how the birds reacted.

Insects see light very differently than humans do. For example, bees can see ultraviolet (UV) light, whereas humans can't. Colors therefore look very different from a bee's point of view. These photos show how humans see a yellow iris flower versus how bees see the same flower.
KLAUS-RUDOLPH LUNAU

On overcast days, sunlight still gets through the clouds, and it creates a pattern that is invisible to humans. But insects like bees and ants can see the pattern, and they use it to figure out direction.

In autumn, monarch butterflies use the sun, Earth's magnetic field and likely other cues to fly about 3,000 miles (about 4,800 kilometers) from Canada and the United States to Mexico, where they spend the winter.
YHELFMAN/GETTY IMAGES

Earth's Magnetic Field

Humans can't sense it, but some animals, especially those that migrate, are able to detect changes in the angle of Earth's *magnetic field* as they travel. What would it be like to sense that field? Would it feel like a gentle tug? Something else?

Landmarks

What if a gust of wind shoves a bee off her path? What if a rabbit runs off its homeward route to escape from a predator? It turns out many animals rely on *landmarks*—reliable objects, like trees, rocks or buildings, that trigger an animal's memories to remember where to go. In 2015 researcher David Pritchard and his team trained wild rufous hummingbirds near the Rocky Mountains to drink sugary water (which mimics flower nectar) out of one of 95 holes drilled in a board. They placed three bottle caps on the board to act as landmarks to help the hummingbirds find the hole. Once the birds learned where the nectar-filled hole was, the scientists moved the landmarks. Not only did the birds use the bottle caps as landmarks, but different birds used them differently, and how they used them changed over time. What objects might hummingbirds and other animals use as landmarks in the wild? This remains an unanswered question.

This ruby-throated hummingbird might remember landmarks in its environment so it can return to find good patches of flowers.
MIKE BONS/GETTY IMAGES

For centuries, humans and other animals have used the stars to navigate.
ANDREY PROKHOROV/SHUTTERSTOCK.COM

Scientists have discovered that rufous hummingbirds have excellent spatial memory.
T.A. HURLY

Clark's nutcrackers can hide thousands of pine seeds in numerous separate locations. Scientists have seen nutcrackers dig straight through the snow and find their hidden food with amazing accuracy. How they manage this great feat is still a mystery to be solved.

PUTTING IT ALL TOGETHER

Next time you are going somewhere, take a minute to stop and think about the cognitive tools *you* use to get around. How do you remember where to go? Do you use beacons, landmarks or different strategies depending on where and how far you are going? Maybe you picture a detailed map of your surroundings. The question of whether animals develop a ***cognitive map*** of their environment is a controversial topic in the animal-cognition field. If animals develop cognitive maps, how detailed are they? Do all animals have cognitive maps? Scientists have been pursuing these questions and arguing about them for decades. Some believe that the most important evidence for cognitive maps is the ability to take a shortcut. In order to calculate a new, shorter route, an animal has to picture the area in their head somehow and then figure out or "see" a shorter path. An example of an animal that can do this is the Egyptian fruit bat.

FRANK FICHTMÜLLER/GETTY IMAGES

Cognitive Maps in Guide Dogs?

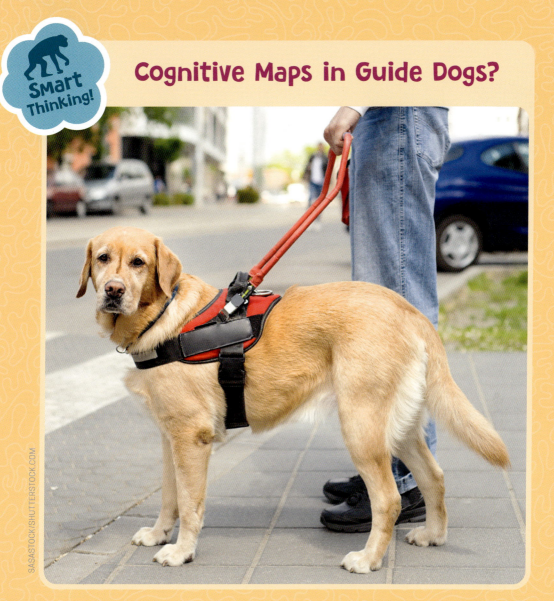

Guide dogs are working dogs who are trained to follow spoken instructions of people with severe visual impairment and lead them safely to where they want to go. In Aix-en-Provence, France, research team Florence Gaunet and Sandie Besse took guide dogs to an area of the city the dogs had never been to before. They walked the dogs on a specific route to find a parked van. After taking this new route *just one time*, the dogs were able later to lead a blindfolded person to the van using a shortcut. The dogs also figured out a detour when a barrier (caution tape) was placed along the route.

Smart Thinking!

Fake Trees and Chickadees

Some birds, like chickadees, spend late summer and fall storing food in many scattered locations so they can retrieve it over the winter. Using coat racks as trees, scientists Megan Thompson and Julie Morand-Ferron at the University of Ottawa gave chickadees the task of finding hidden seeds. Thompson and Morand-Ferron drilled holes in the coat racks and plugged them with cotton balls. The birds had to remember which cotton balls to pluck out to find the seeds. The chickadees showed excellent spatial memory for this task.

SHORTCUT SPECIALISTS

Bats are famous for using *echolocation*—they send out sound waves that bounce off objects, and the returning signals tell the bat where the objects are. Egyptian fruit bats can only sense up to about 100 feet (30 meters) ahead of them, whereas other types of bats can sense objects at a greater distance. Thankfully, Egyptian fruit bats have good vision. When flying long distances, they probably rely mostly on sight to get around. Scientists Ran Nathan and David Shohami and their team in Israel attached trackers to 172 Egyptian fruit bats that lived in the Hula Valley. They collected data over four years and found that many bats took shortcuts between different fruit trees or between fruit trees and their cave.

Another research team, led by Yossi Yovel, found that Egyptian fruit bat pups figured out shortcuts between trees and their cave *after their first day outside*. The scientists sent drones up into the air so they could see what the bat pups saw. Sure enough, they saw some distant large objects, like city buildings, that the bat pups could use as landmarks to help them calculate their shortcuts. After ruling out other cues the bats could have used, such as smell or sound, all evidence suggested that the bats had created cognitive maps of their surroundings and were using them when flying around.

Getting from A to B

What would an Egyptian fruit bat's cognitive map look like? What do they picture in their minds? One thing the scientists pointed out is that even though they found convincing evidence that Egyptian fruit bats use cognitive maps, this doesn't necessarily mean that they use them all the time. They might use one or more of the strategies we

Smart Thinking!

"Snapshots" in Bee Minds?

Bumble bees tend to return to patches of flowers that are good sources of pollen and nectar. Sometimes these patches are spaced widely apart and are a mile or more away from a bee's nest. How does the bee remember how to get to them and how to return home? When a bee first leaves her nest, she tends to circle high above it, flying in bigger and bigger loops. As she ventures farther away, she turns every so often to look back in the direction of her nest. Scientists believe she is forming "snapshot memories" of what her surroundings look like. She will later compare these snapshot memories with what she sees so that she can calculate where to go. This strategy, combined with path integration, allows the bee to navigate without detailed cognitive maps. What's more, over time, with repeated flights between her nest and the flower patches, the bee figures out more efficient routes. Maybe this means cognitive maps aren't necessary to calculate shortcuts? Once again, I am humbled by bumble bees.

Egyptian fruit bats, like this one, can figure out shortcuts, which suggests they may use cognitive maps when they fly.
ANDY ROGERS/FLICKR.COM/CC BY-SA 2.0

saw earlier, like dead reckoning, the stars and/or beacons. If they do, this means they are flexible about what tool they use, basing the choice on the situation.

Thinking back to Charles and other gorillas at the Toronto Zoo and in the wild, do they develop cognitive maps of where they live? If they do, they should be able to figure out shortcuts and approach a remembered location from different directions. How might we be able to see the details of an animal's cognitive map? These are exciting questions that are waiting to be answered. Maybe they will be answered by someone reading this book—someone like you!

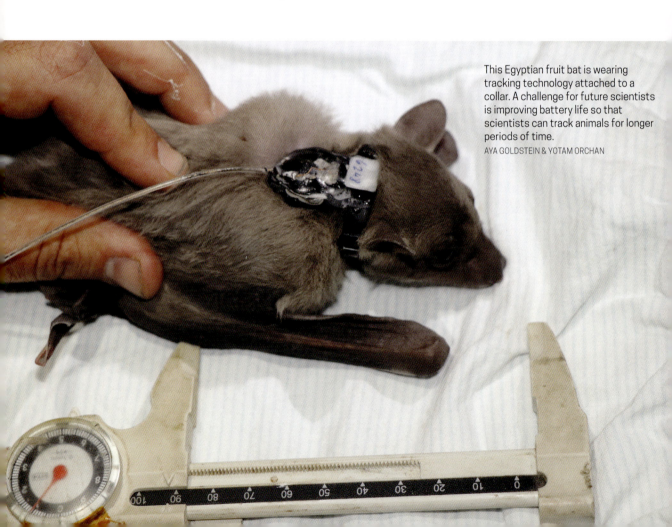

This Egyptian fruit bat is wearing tracking technology attached to a collar. A challenge for future scientists is improving battery life so that scientists can track animals for longer periods of time.
AYA GOLDSTEIN & YOTAM ORCHAN

Smart Thinking!

Charles Henry Turner

THE CRISIS/WIKIMEDIA COMMONS/PUBLIC DOMAIN

In 1932 the Dutch biologist Nikolaas "Niko" Tinbergen discovered that when he moved a circle of pine cones he'd placed around the entrance to a beewolf's nest, the beewolf searched for its nest where the pine cones now were. (A beewolf is a type of solitary wasp whose nest entrance is a tiny hole in the ground.) The beewolf used the pine cones as landmarks. This told Tinbergen that insects—and perhaps many other animals—can learn and think. They might even have a mind. Tinbergen went on to win the Nobel Prize for his research.

However, 24 years before Tinbergen's discovery, Charles Henry Turner reported that burrowing bees could use Coca-Cola bottle caps as landmarks to find their nest entrance. He also suggested that bees might form "memory pictures." He published these findings in a scientific journal, but his breakthroughs were ignored.

Turner was born in Cincinnati, OH, in 1867, two years after slavery ended in the United States. He was the first Black American to earn a PhD at the University of Chicago. After he graduated, no university would hire him, despite his outstanding research and his numerous publications in prestigious journals. He ended up teaching science at a high school for Black students in St. Louis, MO.

Turner continued to study insect behavior. He published over 70 scientific papers and made revolutionary discoveries, such as learning and problem-solving in ants, intelligent web design by spiders, consciousness or "will" in cockroaches and insight in snakes. Now, 100 years after his death, scientists are beginning to acknowledge his work. What would the field of animal cognition look like today if Turner had had the opportunities granted to his white colleagues, or if his research had received the recognition it deserved?

Scientist Spotlight

Suzanne MacDonald

Professor of Psychology
York University, Toronto

Suzanne MacDonald studies animal behavior and has worked with many different species, in the field in Kenya and Canada and in zoos.

When did you first become interested in studying animals? What interests you about them?

Like many people, I have been interested in animals since I was very young. I think that humans are not nearly as fascinating as other species, who have amazing superpowers. They can fly! They can climb! They can survive outside in the winter without a coat!

Do you have a favorite primate that you worked with?

I love them all, really. Charles the gorilla is my absolute favorite and always will be. He is a particularly good artist and even had a gallery showing in New York City! I love all the orangutans—they are a pleasure to hang out with because they are always working on something, trying to figure things out, and they also have a great sense of humor. They like to take a sip of water in their mouths when you're not looking and then spit it at you as a surprise, just like naughty kids. And then they roll around laughing.

What advice do you have for kids who are interested in studying primates?

One of the best ways to work with primates in the zoo is to become a zookeeper, which is an awesome job. Working with ape species in the wild is difficult, because they are so endangered, but there are opportunities to volunteer at primate sanctuaries around the world. Study science, stay curious, and get some hands-on volunteer experience. The primates need your help!

Suzanne MacDonald also studies how raccoons and other animals co-exist with humans in urban environments.
SUZANNE MACDONALD

When defending their territory, can a pride of lions tell when they are outnumbered?
LAURENCARSE/GETTY IMAGES

3

Easy as 1, 2, 3

Counting in Animals

It was January 1989 in Serengeti National Park, Tanzania. Scientist Karen McComb lifted a large speaker from the back of her Land Rover. She carried it a few steps and then set it on the ground behind a thorn bush. She climbed back into the Land Rover and drove a short distance. She stopped and parked so that she was facing a large expanse of flat land. Lounging about 650 feet (200 meters) away, blending in with the straw-colored grass, was a group (or ***pride***) of four wild female lions.

McComb got her video camera ready, along with her notebook and pen. Then she pressed a button. From the speaker came the sound of soft moaning. Then came a full-throated *ROAR!* Next came a series of grunts and then silence. In a flash, all four lions looked in the direction of the speaker. One of the lions slowly stood up. A second lion stood up. Then another, and another. The lion who first stood up tensely crept forward, her head bowed low. She paused every few steps, listening, and sometimes glanced behind her to check that the other lions were following her. They were. Closer and closer the lions crept toward the speaker.

McComb held her breath. The lions soon passed the speaker, looking around for any sign of the strange intruder they had heard. With a *swish-swish* of her tail and one last look, the leading lion turned around and plodded back to their resting spot. Her pride followed.

FALSE ALARM! JUST A TEST

McComb let out a slow exhale. When the lions were relaxing on the grass again, she slowly drove to the speaker, put it in the back of the Land Rover and drove off in search of the next pride. What was McComb doing? She knew that prides will defend their territory from strangers if they know they can win; otherwise, they will retreat. Can lions tell how many intruders there are by their roars?

McComb decided to find out. Sometimes she played a recording of only one lion roaring, like in the scene just described. Other times she played a chorus of three lions roaring. McComb thought that if a pride heard only one lion roaring, it would be more likely to approach than if it heard three lions roaring. One strange lion is easy for a pride of lions to beat in a fight. However, three intruding lions is more of a challenge. The pride might be hesitant to approach or might not approach at all. It might even run in the opposite direction!

Over two and a half years, McComb played the recordings to 21 different prides across Serengeti National Park. She found that lions were much more cautious about defending their territory when they heard the roars of three lions compared with one. Does this mean lions can count? McComb's experiment shows that somehow lions can distinguish between different numbers of roarers.

"Whoops!" Do Hyenas Count?

JEZ BENNETT/SHUTTERSTOCK.COM

In 2007 and 2008, in the Masai Mara National Reserve in Kenya, scientist Sarah Benson-Amram and her team played audio recordings of one, two or three hyenas giving "whoop" calls. Like lions, wild spotted hyenas live in groups and defend their territory. The wild hyenas could tell when they were outnumbered. They were more cautious to approach when they heard the recorded calls of three hyenas compared with two or one. The hyenas seemed to count the number of "intruders."

Lions could tell the difference between one lion roaring versus three. This suggests lions have some degree of numerical ability.
PETER BETTS/SHUTTERSTOCK.COM

The meadow and yellow tents used by Chittka and Geiger to see if honey bees can "count." LARS CHITTKA

1, 2, 3 IN BEES

Another animal that might need to "count" in its everyday life is the honey bee. Scientists Lars Chittka and Karl Geiger suspected that honey bees count landmarks when returning to a flower patch. They set up a honey bee hive in the center of a large empty meadow, and farther down the meadow, they set up a feeder. Between these two points, they set up a line of huge bright-yellow tents. The bees couldn't miss them. The feeder was halfway between the third and the fourth tent. Would the bees count the tents on their way from their hive to the feeder?

Once the bees began flying back and forth between the hive and the feeder, Chittka and Geiger changed the number of tents and feeders. Sometimes they placed more than three tents between the hive and a feeder, and sometimes they placed fewer. Would the bees always choose the feeder that was after the third tent? Yes! Many bees seemed to use the rule "choose the feeder that comes after the third tent." Like the lions and the hyenas, the bees were keeping track of the number of things.

Then, in 2018, another group of scientists trained honey bees to tell the difference between patterns of two or three pictures of stars, lemons, leaves or flowers. Next, they tested the bees to see if they could tell the difference between higher numbers, such as four and five, or four and six. When there were more than four objects in the patterns, honey bees had trouble telling them apart. So it seems that the honey bees could "count" up to four.

Chittka and Geiger discovered that honey bees could tell the difference between different numbers of dots, stars, lemons, leaves and flowers, but only up to four of these objects at a time.
SLAVICA/GETTY IMAGES

ANIMALS USING NUMBERS

Ai the Chimpanzee

In the 1980s, in Japan, scientist Tetsuro Matsuzawa taught a five-year-old chimpanzee named Ai symbols for different colors and objects. He also taught her the symbols we use for numbers, up to 6.

Ai learned to name not only the number of objects she was shown but also the color of the objects and what the objects were. If someone showed her three red pencils, she pressed the buttons on her keyboard for *red*, *pencil* and *3*. Ai was able to name the number, color and object of 300 different combinations!

Ai using a computer touch screen to match "blue" with the correct kanji symbol.
TETSURO MATSUZAWA

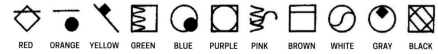

Sheba the Chimpanzee

Also in the 1980s, in the United States, a five-year-old chimpanzee named Sheba was being taught numbers. For example, if someone showed Sheba three apples, she learned to point to a card with *3* on it. Sheba was taught numbers from zero to four, using many different kinds of objects. Then she was given a game to play. The scientists, Sarah Boysen and Gary Berntson, hid oranges in three different spots in a room. Sheba had to find the oranges. After she found them, she had to choose the card that showed the total number of oranges she had found. Right from the start, Sheba moved around the room, found the oranges and then picked the card with the correct number.

Then the scientists made Sheba's game harder. They replaced the oranges with cards that had a number on them. They hid two cards, and Sheba had to find them. When she returned to her starting point, she had to choose a card with the correct sum. For example, if Sheba found one card with *2* and another card with *1*, when she returned to her starting position she had to choose a card with *3*, since two plus one equals three. Sheba aced this game as well. Without any training or help, she collected the cards and then chose the correct sum.

These are some of the symbols Ai was taught to represent various objects, colors and numbers. The symbols were on buttons on a keyboard that was attached to a computer. When Ai chose a symbol by pressing its button, the button lit up.
SOURCE: MATSUZAWA, T. USE OF NUMBERS BY A CHIMPANZEE. *NATURE* 315, 57–59 (1985)

Ai the chimpanzee, Tetsuro Matsuzawa, and Ai's son, Ayumu.
AKIHIRO HIRATA

Alex has to make a choice during an experiment.
ARLENE LEVIN-ROWE

Alex the Parrot

Chimpanzees are not the only animals that can use numbers. Alex, an African gray parrot, was trained by scientist Irene Pepperberg and her team to say the correct number (up to eight) when someone showed him a bunch of objects and asked how many there were. For example, they asked Alex, "How many yellow block?" or "How many green cup?" Once Alex passed these tests, he was given a completely new task. On a tray were three upside-down cups. Alex watched as the scientist lifted each cup one at a time. Under each cup Alex saw a number of his favorite treats—jelly beans, candy hearts, pieces of nuts, crackers or pasta. After replacing the last cup, the scientist asked, "How many total?" In order to say the right answer, Alex had to add up the number of treats under each cup. (The answer was always six or less.) He did it!

Next the scientist showed Alex the tray with two upside-down cups. Under each this time was a plastic number (from one to five) like the ones you can stick on a refrigerator. As before, the scientist lifted up the cups one at a time to show Alex what was underneath. After setting down the second cup, the scientist asked, "How many total?" Alex had to add the numbers in his head. (The answer was always eight or less.) Alex was able to do this too! He made only a small number of mistakes, and when he was asked a second time, he always gave the correct answer.

All these experiments caused quite a splash. Lions, hyenas, chimpanzees, parrots and honey bees can count? Many scientists couldn't believe it. It led to more questions. Were the animals *really* counting? Are animals capable of thinking about abstract things like numbers? What does it mean to count anyway?

Irene Pepperberg purchased Alex the parrot from a Chicago pet store in 1977. He later became one of the most famous parrots in history for showing how birds can think. Sadly, Alex passed away unexpectedly in 2007 from natural causes. Pepperberg established the Alex Foundation, where she continues to study African gray parrots.

Irene Pepperberg giving Alex a task to do during an experiment.
ARLENE LEVIN-ROWE

WHAT DOES IT MEAN TO COUNT?

In 1978 scientists Rochel Gelman and Charles Randy Gallistel tried to pick apart what human children do when they learn to count. They found that children pass through five phases, or what the scientists call "principles."

ONE-TO-ONE CORRESPONDENCE	You can label each item with what is called a **numeric tag**. The numeric tag for each item is different, like 1, 2, 3, etc. You know to tag each item once and only once during a counting event.
STABLE ORDER	You use the numeric tags in the same order each time. For example, you always tag items in the order 1, 2, 3, and never 2, 3, 1.
ORDINALITY	When you use the numeric tags in the same order each time, you know each item's place in the group—first, second, third, etc. This allows you to make judgments such as "more," "less," "bigger" and "smaller."
CARDINALITY	You realize that the last numeric tag used when counting is special, because it tells you the total number of items in the group. This allows you to answer the question, How many?
ABSTRACTION	You can count anything that can be separated, using the previous four principles. For example, jelly beans, coins and burps are all countable things.

Scientists wondered if animals pass through the same phases too. In the experiment with the lions, we don't know whether the lions gave each roar they heard a unique "tag" in their heads. Likewise, were the honey bees somehow mentally tagging each tent they flew past? The lions and bees certainly showed evidence of what is called *ordinality*, because they could make judgments about "more" or "less" roars or tents. Here's an interesting question: Did the lions and bees need to pass through the first two steps before they were able to show ordinality?

In other words, is assigning each roar or tent a special tag necessary in order to tell the difference between "more" and "less"? After all, the five principles are based on what we know about counting in *humans*. Maybe animals decide whether something is "more" or "less" with some other strategy besides using numbers or other symbols.

Something Just "Clicks"

When it comes to the chimpanzees Ai and Sheba, and Alex the parrot, they certainly showed behaviors that match the five counting principles. However, they needed lots of training before they were able to do their impressive counting and mathematical feats. Like, *lots* of training. Sometimes years. Kids also need a few years to learn how to count, but at some point, after learning a few numbers, something just "clicks" in their minds, and they can count any number of items. Kids eventually realize that 50 comes after 49, or that 50 is one more than 49. No one needs to actually show them 49 objects and then add one more to make 50. Animals don't show an aha moment when they understand all numbers and can count with no upper limit. Animals need to be taught every single number. Seriously. Every. Single. Number. So although Ai, Sheba and Alex are certainly superstars, they have limited concepts of number and counting (at least in terms of how humans define those concepts).

When fish that swim in groups (shoals) are allowed to choose between groups that differ in number, many species choose the larger groups over the smaller ones. Perhaps this ability to distinguish between "less" and "more" prompts fish to join bigger groups that provide more protection from predators.

RICH CAREY/SHUTTERSTOCK.COM

To get a treat, Sedona had to knock over the box with the largest number of shapes. She could tell the difference between different pairs of numbers ranging from 1 to 9, and she could choose which of the two numbers was bigger.
KRISTA MACPHERSON

Primates such as monkeys and chimpanzees can be taught to use touch screens with their fingers to make choices between different quantities of things. Animals such as dogs, wolves and bears can be taught to tap the screen with their noses.

"MORE" OR "LESS"

After the early studies with lions, honey bees and chimpanzees, research on whether animals could count shifted a bit. By the early 2000s, the focus changed to whether animals can tell the difference between "more" and "less." (This is included in the *ordinality* phase.) Perhaps animals don't use the same number and counting system that humans do, but they might pay attention to the "how much" of things. This makes sense because animals can choose trees that have more leaves for them to eat, keep track of all of their babies or decide whether they are outnumbered by intruders.

Scientists named the ability to tell the difference between "more" and "less" ***relative quantity judgments***. As we saw, lions and honey bees seem to be able to make relative quantity judgments. What about other animals?

It turns out we are surrounded by all kinds of different animals that can make relative quantity judgments—elephants, dogs, wolves, bears, many species of monkeys, giraffes, spiders and fish, just to name a few. When given the choice between two groups of items, animals are very good at choosing the group that has more. Sometimes animals can be trained to resist the urge to choose the bigger quantity and instead choose the group that has fewer things.

Fiona Cross discovered that Portia africana, a type of jumping spider, can "count" the number of prey using the categories "1" and "2." For numbers 3 and higher, the spiders put them into a category Cross calls "many."
FIONA CROSS

Honey Bees: Mini Mathematicians?

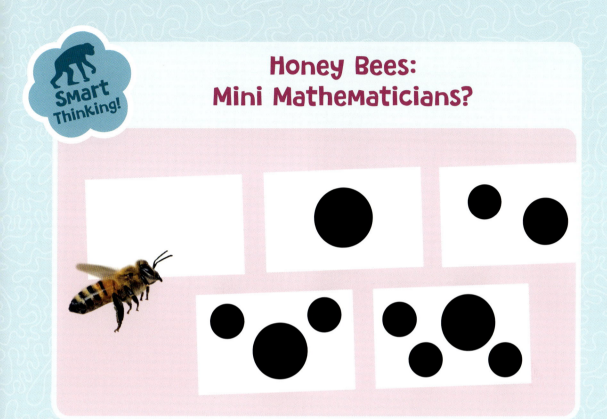

Honey bees might understand the concept of zero. In 2018 a group of scientists in Australia showed honey bees pairs of patterns with one to four black circles, squares and diamonds on a white background. The honey bees were taught to always choose the pattern that had the lowest number of shapes. Then the bees were given a choice between one shape and a blank background, which the bees had never seen before. The bees chose the blank background. The bees seemed to understand that "nothing" was less than one.

Honey bees also can learn symbols that represent numbers. For example, they can learn that an upside-down *T* stands for two, and the letter *N* stands for three. They can do math too. Scientists presented honey bees pairs of patterns that had one, two, four or five shapes in each. The bees were taught that if the two patterns were blue, the bees had to add the shapes. If the two patterns were yellow, the bees had to subtract the shapes. The bees were able to "add" and "subtract" with patterns with up to five shapes.

Clever Hans: A Horse Who Made History

In the early 1900s in Germany, huge crowds gathered to watch a horse named Clever Hans. His owner, Wilhelm von Osten, asked Clever Hans questions such as "How many people have umbrellas?" If there were five people in the crowd who had umbrellas, the horse would tap his foot five times. Von Osten asked him addition, subtraction, multiplication and division questions. Clever Hans gave the correct answer each time. He could even do fractions! The public was astounded. Newspaper headlines bellowed that Clever Hans could do everything but talk.

Some people were skeptical, however, including a scientist named Oskar Pfungst. After observing Clever Hans, Pfungst discovered that the horse had been watching for barely noticeable cues that people (including Von Osten) didn't know they were giving. When the horse saw people tilting their head, tensing their neck muscles or scrunching their eyebrows, he knew to stop tapping his foot. If he couldn't see any people, he tapped the wrong answer. Clever Hans didn't seem so clever after all.

Or was he? He was certainly clever enough to figure out how to answer Von Osten's questions correctly. And he also changed science forever. The term **Clever Hans effect** is used to describe the unintentional influence of scientists on how animals, and even people, react during experiments. Thanks to Clever Hans, scientists now try to make sure they don't give any cues about what they expect or hope will happen. They don't allow the animals to see any humans during their tests, for example, or if people need to be present during the tests, they are unaware of the expected outcomes. Thank you, Clever Hans, for helping us do better science!

SCIENTIFIC METHOD

Scientists begin with a mystery to be solved or a question to be answered. They seek out clues and evidence by observing and running experiments, and then they try to solve the mystery. This "detective work" is called the *scientific method*.

- MAKE AN OBSERVATION
- ASK A QUESTION
- DEVELOP A HYPOTHESIS OR PREDICTION
- TEST THE PREDICTION
- ANALYZE RESULTS
- RECORD THE RESULTS AGAINST HYPOTHESIS
- MAKE A CONCLUSION

African elephants Tara and Kelly at Zoo Atlanta in Georgia watched as a person dropped pieces of carrot or rutabaga one at a time into two barrels. The elephants were very good at choosing the barrel that had more food in it.
BONNIE PERDUE

WHAT'S THE VERDICT? CAN ANIMALS COUNT?

Animals are good at choosing "more" over "less," but they do have a limit. They tend to be much better at telling the difference between two small groups of items than two large groups of items. For example, it is generally easier for animals to tell the difference between 1 versus 6 than 12 versus 18. It is also easier for them if the difference between the groups is large. For instance, they generally have an easier time identifying 2 versus 6 (a difference of 4) than 5 versus 6 (a difference of 1).

These limits make sense if we think of them from the animal's point of view. Choosing a tree that has 10 fruits over a tree that has 2 fruits means that the animal can have a better meal. However, if one tree has 10 fruits and another has 11 fruits, it doesn't really matter which tree the animal picks. The difference is not very big, and whichever tree the animal chooses, they will get a lot of fruit.

So can animals count? The answer so far is yes and no. They certainly have a sense of number, and they can use this sense to help them make decisions in the wild. Some animals, like chimpanzees and parrots, can even learn our number system and do simple math. However, by the time human children are six or seven years old, they leave other animals in the dust. We still don't know all the details about how children learn to count. It's fascinating how other animals can teach us about counting and about ourselves.

Animals can help us appreciate how complex the process of learning to count is.
STOCKPLANETS/GETTY IMAGES

Scientist Spotlight

Álvaro Caicoya

PhD in animal behavior and welfare
University of Barcelona

Álvaro Caicoya studies cognition in giraffes and other ungulates (animals with hooves).

What is it like to work with giraffes?

Giraffes are very peaceful, and they are very attentive to humans. If I am there to do some tasks with them, they will spend a complete hour with me.

Do the giraffes ever do anything funny?

When I arrive at the facilities at the zoo, normally I don't directly start working with them, because I have to take out the tripod, camera, prepare everything, cut carrots or whatever. And they will come behind me, like pushing me towards them to say, "Oh man, please give me carrots already! I'm hungry!" Or they would kick the door to make some sound. And they would do that only if I was there preparing the stuff. It's like they are saying, "Okay, hurry up! I want the task to begin."

Has anything about your research surprised you?

When you start something that no one has done before, you always think, Okay, if no one has done this before, there must be a reason for it. It is not going to work. But from the beginning the giraffes were attentive. They came. They made selections. On maybe their second day they would approach me and take food from me. I think that's the biggest discovery. This kind of animal can do these kinds of tasks and be good models and good subjects.

What would you like people to know about giraffes?

That they are very attentive. And they are more intelligent than we think they are.

4

Figure It Out!
Animals Solving Puzzles

In 2014 researcher Annie Hepp set up a puzzle. First she tied one end of a piece of string around a chunk of raw chicken about the size of a walnut. Then she tied the other end of the string around a wooden perch. The chunk of chicken hung from the perch. Hepp watched and waited. Suddenly a huge black bird with a bald, hot-pink head swooped through the air. Landing gracefully on the perch, it tucked its magnificent wings against its body and paused. It turned its head so that one eye focused on the dangling morsel of meat. C'mon, buddy, Hepp thought. Can you figure out how to get the meat?

Hepp watched as the bird—a turkey vulture named Judge Dredd—reached down and nibbled at the string. With the string still in his beak, he teased it up, which raised the chunk of meat closer toward him. Hepp held her breath. Judge Dredd continued to work the string up through his beak, little by little. This lifted the meat higher and higher. As the meat rose, the string disappeared into Judge Dredd's beak. It looked like he was swallowing the string. Hepp realized he was not swallowing the string but rather gathering the string in his *crop* (a muscular pouch in a bird's throat that is used to store food). Soon Judge Dredd pulled the meat up high enough that he could place it on the perch. Holding the meat down with one foot, he maneuvered his beak like a skilled surgeon to swiftly untie his prize. A few nibbles and gulps later, the meat had disappeared into Judge Dredd's belly. He had solved the puzzle. Bravo, Hepp thought. She was very impressed.

INNOVATIVE VULTURES

Together with scientists Jane Watson and Eric Demers, Hepp gave the same string-pulling test to five other turkey vultures. Three of them didn't solve it—Vladimir and Igor, two turkey vultures at the North Island Wildlife Recovery Centre in Errington, British Columbia, and Jury, a turkey vulture at Pacific Northwest Raptors, an education center and sanctuary for birds of prey in Duncan, British Columbia. Vladimir and Igor avoided the string, whereas Jury approached it but then jumped away. None of the birds had seen raw meat dangling from a string before. Hepp, Watson and Demers thought that maybe these three turkey vultures were too nervous about this new, strange thing in their enclosure to explore it.

However, as we saw, Judge Dredd wasn't nervous and solved the puzzle. He lived at the Raptors with another turkey vulture named Phoenix. Phoenix solved the puzzle too, after he stood beside Judge Dredd and watched how he did it. Frank, a turkey vulture who lived at Grouse Mountain Refuge for Endangered Wildlife in Vancouver, also solved the puzzle. Both Frank and Judge Dredd spent about four to six minutes exploring the string before they

In the 1990s, in one of the earliest string-pulling experiments with birds, scientist Bernd Heinrich suspended dried meat from a string and watched ravens figure out how get the meat. As they pulled up the string with their beaks, the birds tucked the string under one foot. As scavengers, ravens and turkey vultures might have adapted their natural behavior of pulling at the guts of carcasses to solve the string-pulling test.

Annie Hepp and a turkey vulture. In Hepp's experiment, turkey vultures might have adapted their natural behavior of pulling at the intestines and other guts of carcasses to solve the string-pulling test.
LIANE MORRISETTE

figured out how to raise the meat. After all three vultures had solved the puzzle once, they did it much faster when they were given the puzzle again.

Hepp and her team were most impressed by *how* the turkey vultures solved the puzzle. Usually birds solve it by using their beak to pull the string up little by little and tucking the string under one foot. Eventually, step by step, they gather more and more string under their foot and raise the tasty morsel high enough that they can reach down and eat it. Turkey vultures have large, flat, webbed feet that make this technique difficult. This was the first time that birds had used a different strategy—using the tongue to pull the string through their beak and storing the string in their crop.

Leopards were not quite as good as hyenas and lions at solving Borrego's puzzle boxes.
NATALIA BORREGO

Leopards get together to mate, and mother leopards spend time raising their cubs. Other than that, the rest of their lives are solo. It's the same with tigers. Their independent lives are interrupted only to mate and, for mothers, take care of their cubs.

PUZZLE BOXES

To get a glimpse into how animals think, scientists have given animals puzzles to solve that they wouldn't normally encounter in the wild. With a puzzle box, the animal has to figure out how to open the box to get the food inside. Between 2012 and 2015 scientist Natalia Borrego gave puzzle boxes to hyenas, lions, leopards and tigers that lived in zoos and sanctuaries. She suspected that compared with leopards and tigers, who live solitary lives, hyenas and lions might be better at solving puzzle boxes because they live in groups. Groups provide extra daily challenges and stimulation. The animals have to share space and food, know how to interact and communicate peacefully with others, know their "rank" and resolve any disagreements. As a result of this extra mental activity, social carnivores might have evolved to think differently from solitary ones.

A Group Advantage

What was Borrego's puzzle box like? First she wanted the animals to figure out the trick to open it, not smash the box to bits. (But in fairness, smashing the box open is one way to solve it.) So she made the puzzle box out of material that boats are made of—a flexible StarBoard marine-grade polymer. To get at the chunk of raw meat inside, the animals had to pull on a short rope attached to a spring that would open the door. Borrego drilled holes into the sides of the box so the animals could easily see and smell the meaty treat inside. She placed the box on the ground in each of the animals' enclosures three times. Each time she gave them 10 minutes to solve it. What happened?

Borrego was correct. The social animals were better at solving the puzzle box than the solo-living animals. Hyenas were the best at solving it, followed by lions and then leopards and tigers. Hyenas and lions also spent more time trying to figure out the puzzle box before giving up.

Smart Thinking!

A Different Perspective

Animal-cognition scientists try to look at things from the animal's point of view. Imagine you can see your favorite food, but it is out of reach. There are weird-looking objects nearby that you've never seen before. Should you touch them? Can they help you reach the food? Maybe the food is in a peculiar-looking box, but you've never seen a box before. To solve these puzzles, you have to overcome any fear of the new objects and explore how they work. Some animals may not solve puzzles because they are too scared of new objects humans give them.

A lion solving Borrego's puzzle box.
NATALIA BORREGO

A wild elephant solving one of Jacobson's puzzle boxes.
COMPARATIVE COGNITION FOR CONSERVATION LAB AT HUNTER COLLEGE

More Brainteasers

Scientists have given puzzle boxes to a variety of different animals. Sarah Jacobson and her team recently gave them to elephants. Each animal had to use its trunk to slide the top door, pull the middle door and push the bottom door to get either a biscuit or marshmallows. All the elephants solved at least one type of door, and over half of them solved all three.

Primates also have been given puzzle boxes to solve. In Gibraltar, in 2017 and 2018, Frederica Amici and her team studied a group of wild, free-ranging Barbary macaques (monkeys). The scientists gave the macaques three different puzzle boxes to solve. With the first box, the macaques had to rotate the lid to get the peanut inside. With the second box, they had to pull on a tab to make the peanut fall out. With the third, they had to use a stick to push the peanut through a hole. Six out of 15 macaques solved at least one of the puzzles. The macaques showed a lot of individual differences in their strategies, including the alpha male, who preferred to watch the other macaques do the work.

THE FLOATING OBJECT TASK

In the floating object task, a reward such as a peanut sits at the bottom of a transparent tube. To get the peanut, the animal has to spit water into the tube. The more water the animal spits into the tube, the higher the peanut rises. With enough water, the peanut floats to the top of the tube where the animal can reach it.

Scientists have given the floating object task to a variety of apes, such as gorillas, chimpanzees and orangutans. The results have been mixed. Sometimes the apes solved the task, and sometimes they didn't. Some apes

Denda, an orangutan at the Seneca Park Zoo in Rochester, NY, spits water into the tube to make the peanut rise up high enough for him to reach it. He solved the task the first time he was given it.
CAROLINE DELONG

solved it the first time they encountered it. More often, though, the apes first tried different, unsuccessful strategies to get at the peanut. As a hint, scientists sometimes put a bit of water in the tube so the apes could see the peanut floating on top of the water. Some primates then spat more water into the tube. Others still couldn't figure it out. But they're not alone. Many human children under the age of eight can't solve this task by themselves.

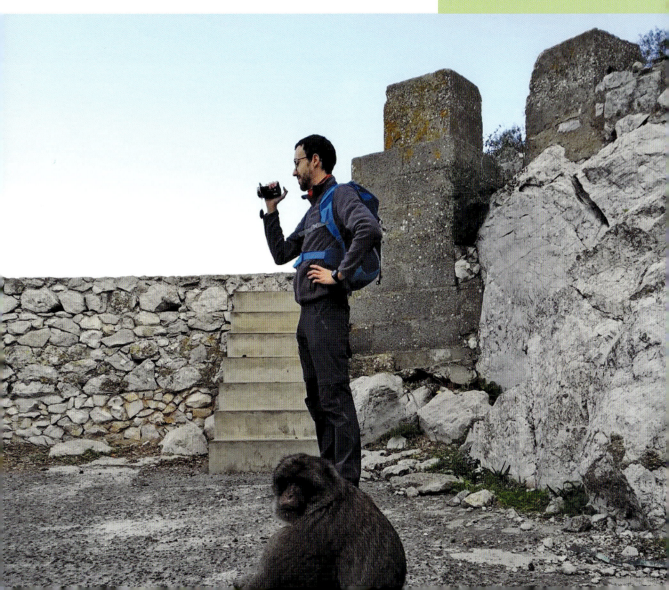

During Amici's experiment, an alpha male lay down beside research team member Álvaro Caicoya while the other macaques solved the puzzles.
ANA BELÉN NIEMBRO

Elephants in Barrett and Benson-Amram's experiment preferred marshmallows over peanuts. Here, Chandra (with her niece Achara watching) is trying to solve the task. LISA P. BARRETT

Sometimes animals have solved puzzles using strategies that scientists didn't anticipate. Kumang, an orangutan at the Seneca Park Zoo in New York, first tried to solve the floating object task with a peanut, by using sticks and pieces of hay as chopsticks. She eventually spat some water into the tube and scooped out the peanut with cardboard. The second time the elephant Shanthi encountered the tube, she added one squirt of water from her trunk and then shot the marshmallow out of the tube by blowing air at it!

In 2017 scientists Lisa Barrett and Sarah Benson-Amram gave the floating object task to elephants at the Smithsonian's National Zoological Park in Washington, DC, and the Oklahoma City Zoo. The reward was a marshmallow. The puzzle seemed difficult for the elephants to solve. However, one elephant, Shanthi, solved the task by blowing water from her trunk into the tube. Zookeepers often saw Shanthi playing with water, so maybe this gave her an advantage in a task that involved water as the solution. Barrett and Benson-Amram suspect that apes may have an easier time solving the floating object task because, unlike elephants, they often use tools to get food.

THE AESOP'S FABLE TASK

Some animals are unable to spit or pour water into tubes, so scientists have modified the task. They give the animals (mostly birds) a container with a bit of water on the bottom and a treat that floats on the surface of the water. To reach the treat, the animal has to drop stones or other objects into the container to make the water rise high enough for them to reach the floating treat. This task is named after the Aesop's Fable "The Crow and the Pitcher," in which a thirsty crow drops pebbles into a pitcher of water until the water level is high enough for him to take a drink.

Sometimes scientists make the task even trickier by giving the animal a choice of objects that will either sink or float. Corvids, which are birds such as rooks, New Caledonian crows and Eurasian jays, usually solve the task if they first learn that stones can be dropped into tubes.

A New Caledonian crow dropping stones into a tube during the Aesop's Fable task.
DR. SARAH JELBERT

These lemurs are tasked with figuring out how to get food out of this dispenser.
MONIQUE SIEBEN / EYEEM/GETTY IMAGES

Smart Thinking!

Zoos versus the Field

How are research results from zoos different from those from the field? Zoo animals are still wild animals, but they live in much simpler environments. This is an advantage because it's easier to observe them and scientists have more control over their environment. Scientists don't have to chase after an animal if it runs or flies away, and they don't have to worry about other species interfering in their experiment. Scientists can also know more about the life history of the animal. Field studies, however, have the advantage of showing how animals behave in their natural environment. This might be quite different from how they behave in a zoo. Scientists have to weigh these factors when designing their research. Some research lends itself more to zoos, and others to fieldwork. It also depends on what research question the scientists are asking.

A raccoon solving the Aesop's Fable task the traditional way: (1) collect stones, (2) place them on the platform and push them into the tube, and (3) reach in and grab the treat.
LAUREN STANTON

Researcher Lauren Stanton and her team recently gave the Aesop's Fable task to raccoons at the USDA National Wildlife Research Center in Fort Collins, Colorado. They built a platform around the top of a tube and placed stones on top of it. A marshmallow cut into small pieces was the reward floating on the bit of water at the bottom of the tube. The raccoons had to knock stones into the tube to raise the water so that they could reach the marshmallow bits. The racoons also had access to other objects that Stanton and her team provided: balls that floated on water and a small cup. Two raccoons eventually learned to knock stones into the water, but other raccoons tried different methods. One raccoon gripped the rim of the tube with her front paws, rocked her body back and forth and tipped the tube over, spilling the marshmallow pieces where she could reach them. Two other raccoons dropped balls into the tube and pushed them down over and over, which splashed the bits of marshmallow up where they could grab them. Two other raccoons dropped a small cup into the tube, waited while the marshmallow bits floated into the cup and then yanked the cup out before it sank.

WINDOWS INTO OTHER MINDS

Watching an animal solve a puzzle allows us to get into the details of how animals might think. Interestingly, puzzle-solvers are often animals who have had previous experience with some part of the solution. Shanthi could sometimes be seen shooting water from her trunk into boxes of food pellets zookeepers placed in her enclosure for enrichment. The vultures and big cats likely had experience pulling at stringlike intestines and other guts when eating other animals. They possibly transferred these experiences to an entirely new situation. However, unsuccessful attempts to solve a puzzle can be just as interesting—or more interesting—as successes. Failures can provide clues to what the animal might have been thinking and what they understood about the situation.

> In some experiments, animals are given special treats like marshmallows. Although the animals find them very yummy, scientists have to follow the zookeepers' rules. Zookeepers monitor the animals' diets very closely, including the number of treats they get. Many treats can make an animal extremely sick, and they might even die. So please leave the feeding and treat-giving to the professionals.

An elephant's flexible trunk allows it to do many things, including solve puzzles.
UDO KIESLICH/GETTY IMAGES

Creating puzzles for animals is also a challenge for scientists. They have to keep in mind what an animal is physically capable of. They also want to include some aspect of the animal's natural environment or encourage natural behaviors. The scientists have to give the animal something that is challenging but not *too* challenging and that will provide some insight into how the animal thinks. They also have to make sure the animal can't destroy the puzzle! This is not necessarily an easy task.

In a sense, all the experiments featured in this book are instances of humans giving animals puzzles to solve. For the animal, the reward for solving the puzzle is a treat, whereas for the humans, the reward is another step toward understanding how the mind of another species works. Perhaps at some level the animals are trying to figure us out too.

Remember the chapter on personality? Some scientists are currently studying the relationship between personality and problem-solving in animals. For example, one hypothesis is that animals that are less fearful of new things and are more persistent might be more successful at solving puzzles.

String-Pulling with Bumble Bees

A team of scientists from the United Kingdom, China and Norway gave bumble bees a version of the string-pulling task. They placed "flowers" (blue discs with a drop of sugar water in their centers) underneath a plexiglass table. To reach the sugar water, using their legs and pincerlike mouthparts, the bees had to pull on a string attached to the disc to move it out from under the table. Two out of 25 bees solved this puzzle. The scientists described the two successful bees as being "exceptionally explorative" with the setup. But that's not all. Other bees learned how to pull the string to get the sugary treat simply by watching "demonstrator" bees do it. And then these bees went on to demonstrate and teach more bees. In this way, the new string-pulling skill spread throughout several colonies (families) of bees. This shows that complex problem-solving and the ability to learn from others doesn't necessarily require a big brain like humans have.

Smart Thinking!

An "Insightful" Chimpanzee

Famous experiments on puzzle-solving in chimpanzees were done in the early 1900s by the psychologist Wolfgang Köhler. He placed food out of the chimpanzees' reach and provided objects nearby that they could use, like sticks and boxes. One chimpanzee, Sultan, kept jumping up at bananas that Köhler had hung out of reach. Sultan eventually stopped and paced back and forth. He then stood in front of a box, grabbed it and placed it under the bananas. Köhler watched as Sultan climbed on top of the box, then jumped up and snatched the bananas. On another occasion Köhler saw Sultan slide one piece of bamboo into another to make a stick long enough to drag a piece of food toward him.

Köhler is well known in the animal-cognition field, not just for these experiments but also for his conclusion that Sultan showed evidence of insight learning. This is when an animal sees a solution, sometimes after a number of unsuccessful attempts—an aha moment. Scientists have debated whether Sultan actually experienced insight and whether animals other than humans are capable of insight. In any event, Köhler and Sultan helped change the way we view chimpanzees.

Smart Thinking!

A Breakthrough with David Greybeard

An important milestone happened in 1960. Scientist Jane Goodall watched as a wild chimpanzee she named David Greybeard sat on a termite mound. He poked a piece of grass into a hole in the mound. He pulled it out and raised the grass to his mouth. Goodall wondered what he was doing. After David Greybeard left, she sat on the mound herself and tried poking grass into the hole. To her surprise, when she pulled it out, it was covered in termites. David Greybeard had used grass to "fish" for termites! Up until then, it was thought that only humans used tools. This was also an incredible example of problem-solving. Since then Goodall and other scientists have witnessed many instances of tool use by chimpanzees and by other animals as well.

THE FUTURE OF ANIMAL COGNITION

The field of animal cognition is vast, and the future of animal cognition is rich and juicy. There is so much more to discover about animal personality, spatial memory, counting and puzzle-solving. Animal-cognition scientists also study many other topics, such as communication, how animals learn from other animals and whether animals can recognize themselves in mirrors. Perhaps you have your own questions that await to be answered.

Technology is also allowing scientists a closer look at how animals think. For example, scientists Jenna Congdon and Suzanne MacDonald are using cameras and computers to track orangutans at the Toronto Zoo 24 hours a day. As I write this book, Congdon is using artificial intelligence (AI) to "teach" the computers to recognize the individual orangutans. One surprise is that the orangutans often face the camera with their rear ends. Who would have thought that science could involve drawing rectangles around footage of orangutan butts? Congdon told me, "They have very different-looking butts, if you pay enough attention." In all seriousness, AI has huge potential to allow scientists to learn new things about the animals they study. Their observations can also be helpful to zookeepers when monitoring the animals' health. The Toronto Zoo plans to use the AI technology with big cats and polar bears too. What will the next generations of animal-cognition scientists uncover about animal minds? I am excited to find out!

In this screenshot from cameras placed in the orangutan enclosure at the Toronto Zoo, Jenna Congdon has drawn rectangles around Budi and Sekali to help the computer to learn to recognize individual orangutans.
DR. MINA HOSSEINI, EAIGLE INC.

Scientist Spotlight

Natalia Borrego

Wildlife biologist

University of Minnesota's Lion Center

Natalia Borrego is also a researcher with the University of Konstanz and the Max Planck Institute of Animal Behavior.

Why are you interested in lions?

Lions are the only social big cats, so that's kind of where I started. I said, "All right, well, let's see how lions do compared to big cats who don't live in groups." Everybody kind of thought that lions were these lazy, not very smart, kind of big brute-force animals. In fact, they are much more switched-on than they seem.

Is it hard to work with lions?

They are really, really good at breaking things. When I make puzzle boxes, it's like it has to be able to be run over by a Mack truck and survive. It was a lot of trial and error to find things that are lion-proof. And nothing is completely lion-proof, so you have to build something so that if they break it, you can fix it. They're also similar to house cats. They have off days where they're cranky and don't feel like participating. Or they can be really excited and be like, "I'm going to keep your research equipment and you can't have it back." I think the longest one lion kept it was three days until I finally managed to get it back.

Is there anything you would like people to know about lions that they might not know?

There's more to them than these big brutes they're made out to be. A lot of people think if you stand in front of a wild lion, it will just attack you. They are actually quite afraid of humans. Obviously, they're a giant wild animal and they should be left alone, but there is something to be appreciated rather than just having a fearful response to them. And I always, always say that there is no Lion King. Lions live as equals.

Natalia has studied lions and other big cats in zoos, sanctuaries and on safaris.
COURTESY OF NATALIA BORREGO

Glossary

animal cognition—the field of science that studies how nonhuman animals think: how they learn, remember, make decisions and solve problems

anthropomorphism—the tendency to see other animals as humans or describe animals using human characteristics

Clever Hans effect—the unintentional influence scientists can have on the way animals and people react during experiments when scientists give subconscious cues about what they expect or hope will happen

cognition—mental processes, including thinking, learning, memory, decision-making and problem-solving

cognitive map—a mental picture or representation of one's surroundings

crop—a muscular pouch in a bird's throat that is used to store food

dead reckoning—the ability of an animal to travel back to its starting point in a relatively straight line, despite having wandered around in various directions beforehand (see *path integration*)

echolocation—the ability of some animals, such as bats and dolphins, to locate distant or invisible objects by sending out sound waves that bounce back from the objects, telling the animal where the objects are

extroverts—individuals who are outgoing, prefer to be around others and feel energized after interacting with them

foragers—individuals who search for and gather food (forage)

introverts—individuals who enjoy being alone, are often quiet when in large groups and feel tired after being around others

landmarks—reliable objects, such as trees or buildings, that remind individuals where they are so they know where to go

magnetic field—the area around a magnetic object that can push another magnetic object away or pull the object toward it. Magnetic fields are created from moving electric charges.

natural selection—Charles Darwin's idea that genetic changes in living things make some individuals more suited to their environment and therefore more likely to survive and reproduce (see *theory of evolution*)

nocturnal animals—animals that are active at night

numeric tag—the unique label someone gives to each item when they are learning to count, such as 1, 2, 3, etc.

path integration—the process by which an animal calculates the distance and direction of all the little paths it took while traveling, to create a straight route back home

personality—human patterns of behavior that are consistent across time and different situations. Other animals have also shown evidence of personality.

pride—a group of lions

relative quantity judgments—the ability to tell the difference between "more" and "less"

search patterns—a memory strategy animals use by continuously moving in a particular way or direction

spatial memory—a form of memory that allows an individual to remember where things are located in the physical environment

theory of evolution—the idea that living things develop and change from previous generations, which happens, according to Charles Darwin, through natural selection

traits—characteristics scientists use to describe personality or individual differences

Resources

PRINT

de Waal, Frans. *Are We Smart Enough to Know How Smart Animals Are?* W.W. Norton & Company, Inc., 2016.

Groc, Isabelle. *Conservation Canines: How Dogs Work for the Environment.* Orca Book Publishers, 2021.

Harrington, Janice N. *Buzzing with Questions: The Inquisitive Mind of Charles Henry Turner.* Calkins Creek, 2019.

Kokias, Kerri. *Clever Hans: The True Story of the Counting, Adding, and Time-Telling Horse.* G.P. Putnam's Sons, 2020.

Montgomery, Sy. *The Octopus Scientists: Exploring the Mind of a Mollusk.* HMH Books for Young Readers, 2015.

Ottaviani, Jim. *Primates: The Fearless Science of Jane Goodall, Dian Fossey, and Biruté Galdikas.* Square Fish, 2015.

Spinner, Stephanie. *Alex the Parrot: No Ordinary Bird (A True Story).* Alfred A. Knopf, 2012.

Turner, Pamela S. *Crow Smarts: Inside the Brain of the World's Brightest Bird.* HMH Books for Young Readers, 2016.

Vanderklugt, Kyla. *Science Comics: Crows; Genius Birds.* First Second, 2020.

Wyman, Janet. *Eight Dolphins of Katrina: A True Tale of Survival.* HMH Books for Young Readers, 2013.

ONLINE

Alex Foundation: Learn more about Alex the parrot and Irene Pepperberg's work at alexfoundation.org.

Animal Cognition: Find a variety of articles about animal cognition, and interviews with scientists, at animalcognition.org.

Bat Lab for Neuro-Ecology: Learn more about bat-navigation research at yossiyovel.com.

Brown Dog Lab: Dig deeper into dog cognition at sites.brown.edu/browndoglab and at the **Canine Cognition Center**, doglab.yale.edu.

"Bumblebees learned to pull strings for reward": A video showing bumble bees in the string-pulling experiment can be found at youtube.com/watch?v=gSCr5OxXN1A.

Doctor Spider: Fiona Cross is known as "Doctor Spider." You can learn more about her research at doctorspider.net.

Movement Ecology Lab: Read more research on the movement of bats and other animals at huji.move-ecol.com.

Primate Portal: A group of scientists is studying the minds of baboons at the Seneca Park Zoo. Find out more at theprimateportal.org.

Suzanne Macdonald: To learn about MacDonald's recent research with animals, both in zoos and in the wild, visit suzannemacdonald.ca.

Links to external resources are for personal and/or educational use only and are provided in good faith without any express or implied warranty. There is no guarantee given as to the accuracy or currency of any individual item. The author and publisher provide links as a service to readers. This does not imply any endorsement by the author or publisher of any of the content accessed through these sites.

Acknowledgments

My heartfelt thanks go to all the scientists who appear throughout this book. Your research is so exciting and I had so much fun writing about it. Thank you for answering all my questions, reading what I wrote and providing feedback to make sure I got the details right. It is an honor to feature your hard work and dedication that allow us to further understand and appreciate the other creatures with whom we share this planet.

To all the scientists and to the staff at zoos that kindly shared their photos with me: Thank you for searching through your files to find them and for being willing to share them with my readers. A special thanks to Natalia Borrego, Álvaro Caicoya and Lauren Highfill, who supported this project from the very beginning.

To my agent, Stacey Kondla: I am so grateful we are a team. I deeply appreciate your hard work, dedication and support, and our mutual love of and excitement for science and all living things.

To Kirstie Hudson, my editor at Orca Book Publishers: It was such a joy to work with you on this book. Thank you for believing in my manuscript and for helping me to make it shine brighter.

Many thanks to the entire Orca team: copyeditor Vivian Sinclair, for her sharp eye and curiosity; designer Jenn Playford, for making it all look so beautiful; and editorial assistant Georgia Bradburne, who worked her magic behind the scenes to make it all come together.

Michael Beran, Jenna Congdon, Sarah Benson-Amram and Catherine Plowright kindly agreed to read and provide feedback on my entire first draft. I am sincerely grateful for your time, thoughtful suggestions, support and enthusiasm for this book.

Researching and writing this book brought back so many fond memories of being a student in "The Bee Lab." Thank you to Catherine Plowright, France Landry, Ginny Simonds, Dalit Weinberg and all of the former students we worked with for making graduate school such an enjoyable experience. Catherine, I will always be grateful for your wise, gentle guidance and for introducing me to the world of animal cognition.

As always, my family has been a constant source of support, love and encouragement. Thank you especially to Stephen, Lelynd and Lexi for your laughter, love and adventures. Spirit, you were on my mind so often while I wrote this book. Thank you for being a constant connection to the nonhuman world and for being an overall wonderful dog.

Last, but certainly not least, this book is dedicated to Cecilia (Cia) Penner. Cia was my high school biology teacher, and she has been my biggest cheerleader ever since. Her belief in me was a game-changer. Over the years her continuous generosity, reassurance, support and faith in what I can accomplish has never ceased to amaze me. Thank you, Cia, from the bottom of my heart, for always being there and for accompanying me on this journey.

This book was written on the Traditional Land of the Attawandaron, Anishinaabe and Haudenosaunee Peoples, and I respectfully acknowledge their Ancestors and Elders, past and present, and the generations to come. I honor the enduring presence and deep Traditional Knowledge, laws and philosophies of the Indigenous Peoples with whom I share these lands today.

Index

Page numbers in **bold** *indicate an image caption.*

Aesop's Fable task, 72–74
Ai the chimpanzee, 50, 51, 55
Alex the parrot, 52–53, 55
Amici, Frederica, 70
amphibians, 16
Anderson, Roland, 6
animal behaviors: alpha male, 70, **71**; anthropomorphism, 20, 82; and captivity, 74; and personality, 16–22; and problem-solving, 61, 74; social structure, 68–69; teaching skills to other animals, 76
animal cognition, 2, 82
animal cognition science: careers in, 2, 22, 42; discrimination, 41; future of, 79; methods, 19, 58, 59, 74, 76
animal welfare, zoos, 18, **19**
anthropomorphism, 20, 82
ants, 33

Barrett, Lisa, 72
bats, 36, 39–40
beacons, 32, 36, 40
bees: bumble, 1–2, 17, 39, 76; burrowing, 41; honey, 48–49, 57; navigation, 32; vision of, **33**
Benson-Amram, Sarah, 46, 72
Berntson, Gary, 51
Besse, Sandie, 37
birds: navigation, 32, 33, 34; numerical ability, 52–53, 55; problem-solving, **64**, 65–67, 72–73; spatial memory, 36, 38
Borrego, Natalia, 68–69, 80, **81**
Boysen, Sarah, 51
butterflies, 32, **34**

Caicoya, Álvaro, 62, **63**, **71**
captivity: animal welfare, 18, **19**; and natural behaviors, 74
cats, domestic, **7**, 16
cats, wild: numerical ability, **44**, 45–46, **47**; problem-solving, 68–69, 80, **81**; traits, 16, **21**
Charles the gorilla, 9, 25–27, 29, 32, 40, 42
chickadees, 38
chimpanzees: numerical ability, 50–51, 55; problem-solving, 70, 77, 78; traits, 16
Chittka, Lars, 48, **49**
Clever Hans effect, 58, 82
cognition, defined, 2, 82
cognitive maps, 36, 37, 39, 40, 82
Congdon, Jenna, 79
counting principles, 54–55, 60–61
Cross, Fiona, **56**
crows, **64**, 73

Darwin, Charles, 15
dead reckoning, 32, 33, 82
Demers, Eric, 66
dogs: numerical ability, **55**; and personality, **9**, 18, 19; spatial memory, 37; training of, 56; working, 18, 37
dolphins, **10**, 11–15, 22
dung beetles, 32

echolocation, 39–40, 82
elephants, 16, **60**, 70, 72, 75
extroverts, 8, 82

ferrets, **16**
fish, 55
floating object task, 70–72

flowers: and insect's vision, **33**; locating, 1–2, 39
foragers, 2, 82

Gaunet, Florence, 37
Geiger, Karl, 48, **49**
giraffes, 62
Goodall, Jane, 78
gorillas: Charles the gorilla, 9, 25–27, 29, 32, 40, 42; problem-solving, 70; spatial memory, **24**, 29–31, 32, 40; wild, **30**, 31
Grouse Mountain Refuge for Endangered Wildlife, Vancouver (BC), 66

hamsters, 32
Heinrich, Bernd, 66
Hepp, Annie, 65–66, 67
Highfill, Lauren, 11, 13, 14–15, 22, **23**
horses, 58
human: numerical ability, 54–55, 61; personality testing, 6–7, 8; problem-solving, 71
hummingbirds, 32, 34, **36**
Hurricane Katrina, **14**, 15
hyenas, 16, 46, 68–69

insects: behaviors, 41; and dead reckoning, 32, 33; migration, **34**; vision of, **33**. *See also* bees
insight learning, 77
introverts, 8, 82

Jacobson, Sarah, 70
jays, 73

Köhler, Wolfgang, 77
Kuczaj, Stan, 11, 13, 14–15

landmarks, 34, 41, 82
language skills, 50–51
lemurs, 23, 73
leopards, 21, 68–69
lions: numerical ability, 44, 45–46, 47; problem-solving, 68–69, 80, 81; traits, 21

MacDonald, Suzanne, 25–27, 29–31, 42, 43, 79
magnetic fields, 28, 34, 83
Marine Life Oceanarium, Gulfport (MS), 11, 14–15, 22
Mather, Jennifer, 5
Matsuzawa, Tetsuro, 50, 51
McComb, Karen, 45–46
migration: butterflies, 34; sea turtles, 28
monkeys, 16, 70–71
moon/stars navigation, 33, 35
Morand-Ferron, Julie, 38
more-or-less judgments, 45–46, 54–55, 56, 60–61

natural behaviors: and cognition, 20; and problem-solving, 75–76; in the wild, 30, 31, 61
natural selection, 15, 83
navigation methods: cognitive maps, 36, 37, 39, 40, 82; and migration, 28, 34; types of, 32–36, 39–40
nocturnal animals, 33, 83
North Island Wildlife Recovery Centre, Errington (BC), 66
numerical ability: of animals, 53, 54–55, 60–61; of humans, 54–55, 61; more-or-less judgments, 45–46, 54–55, 56, 60–61; testing of, 27, 44, 45–53, 56–58
numeric tag, 54, 83
nutcrackers, 36

octopuses, 4, 5–6
orangutans, 29, 42, 70, 72, 79

Pacific Northwest Raptors, Duncan (BC), 66
parrots, 52–53, 55
path integration, 33, 83
Pepperberg, Irene, 52–53
personality: animal traits, 5–6, 11–22; and behavior over time, 14–15, 17; defined, 6–7, 83; human traits, 6–7, 8; and problem-solving, 76; and social structure, 68–69
pets, 7, 9, 16, 18, 20
Pfungst, Oskar, 58
Pritchard, David, 34
problem-solving: Aesop's Fable task, 72–74; floating object task, 70–72; insight learning, 77; and natural behaviors, 75–76; puzzle-box task, 68–70, 73, 80; string-pulling task, 65–67, 76
puzzle-box task, 68–70, 73, 80

raccoons, 43, 74
ravens, 66
relative quantity judgments, 56, 83. *See also* more-or-less judgments
resources, 84–85
rooks, 73

scientific method: Clever Hans effect, 58; and natural behaviors, 74; process, 19, 59, 76
scientists. *See* animal cognition science
search patterns, 32, 83
sea turtles, 28
Seneca Park Zoo, Rochester (NY), 70, 72
Serengeti National Park, Tanzania, 45–46
Shanthi the elephant, 72, 75
Sheba the chimpanzee, 51, 55
Shohami, David, 39

spatial memory: cognitive maps, 36, 37, 39, 40, 82; defined, 29, 83; and gorillas, 25–27, 29–31; and navigation, 28, 32–40
spiders, 56
Stanton, Lauren, 74
stars/moon navigation, 33, 35
string-pulling task, 65–67, 76
sunlight navigation, 33, 34

technology: artificial intelligence, 79; audio recordings, 45–46; GPS trackers, 28, 39, 40; touch screens, 50, 56
theory of evolution, 15, 83
Thompson, Megan, 38
tigers, 21, 68–69
Tinbergen, Nikolaas "Niko", 41
tools, use of, 77, 78
Toronto Zoo (ON), 9, 25–27, 29–31, 40, 79
traits, defined, 6–7, 83
Turner, Charles Henry, 41

volunteer experience, 22, 42
vultures, turkey, 65–67

wasps, 41
Watson, Jane, 66
wildlife sanctuaries and parks, 45–46, 66, 68

Yovel, Yossi, 39

zoos: animal welfare, 18, 19; and careers in, 42; cognition testing, 9, 25–27, 29–31, 60, 70, 72; and natural behaviors, 74; petting, 3; use of unhealthy treats, 75

89

CHIARA SPARANESE

DANA L. CHURCH is an author and researcher who did her PhD in animal cognition at the University of Ottawa. She is the author of *The Beekeepers: How Humans Changed the World of Bumble Bees*. Dana lives in Waterloo, Ontario.

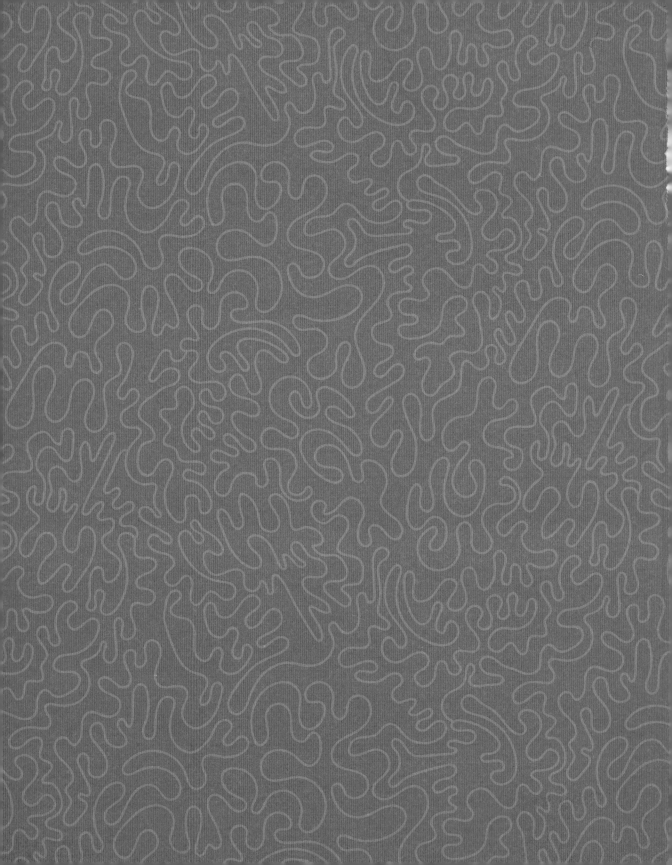